THE
POWER
OF *I AM*

STUDY GUIDE

ALSO BY JOEL OSTEEN

Break Out!
Break Out! Journal
Daily Readings from Break Out!
Every Day a Friday
Every Day a Friday Journal
Daily Readings from Every Day a Friday
I Declare
I Declare Personal Application Guide
The Power of I Am
You Can, You Will
You Can, You Will Journal
Daily Readings from You Can, You Will
Your Best Life Now
Daily Readings from Your Best Life Now
Your Best Life Begins Each Morning
Your Best Life Now Study Guide
Your Best Life Now for Moms
Your Best Life Now Journal
Starting Your Best Life Now

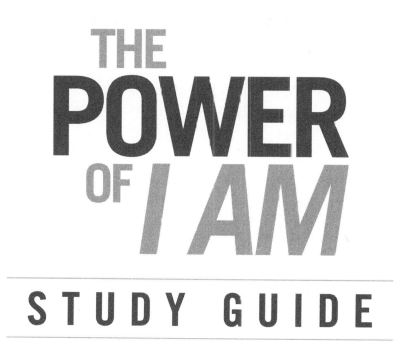

THE POWER OF I AM

STUDY GUIDE

JOEL OSTEEN

FaithWords

New York • Boston • Nashville

One Scripture quotation was taken from the *New King James Version* of the Bible. Copyright © 1982 by Thomas Nelson, Inc. Used by permission. All rights reserved.

One scripture is noted from *The Message*. Copyright © 1993, 1994, 1995, 1996, 2000, 2001, 2002. Used by permission of NavPress Publishing Group.

Literary development and interior design: Koechel Peterson & Associates, Inc., Minneapolis, Minnesota.

FaithWords
Hachette Book Group
1290 Avenue of the Americas
New York, NY 10104
www.faithwords.com

Printed in the United States of America

First Edition: October 2015

10 9 8 7 6 5 4 3 2 1

FaithWords is a division of Hachette Book Group, Inc. The FaithWords name and logo are trademarks of Hachette Book Group, Inc.

The Hachette Speakers Bureau provides a wide range of authors for speaking events. To find out more, go to www.hachettespeakersbureau.com or call (866) 376-6591.

The publisher is not responsible for websites (or their content) that are not owned by the publisher.

ISBN: 978-1-45553-817-1

Contents

Introduction

I'm delighted that you have chosen to use this study guide that was written as a companion to my book *The Power of I Am*. This study is meant to help you think through how the words that you speak about yourself have the power to transform every aspect of your being. The thoughts and questions addressed in the following pages will help you to examine your life and take important steps to become all God has created you to be.

How you use this study guide will depend on the purpose you have in mind. You can work through it on your own for personal development, as a part of a small group/book club, or even during a weekend retreat. The format of each chapter is simple and user-friendly. For maximum benefit, you will first read the chapter from *The Power of I Am,* and then you will work your way through the corresponding chapter in this study guide.

The most effective way to use this study guide is to go through it on your own, even if you're also going to discuss it in a group setting or on a retreat. The majority of the questions are personal, and taking the time to read through the chapters in the book and think through how each question can affect your life will give the study depth and immediate personal application.

Because most of the questions are personal, if you use this study guide in a group setting or on a retreat, remember that courtesy and mutual respect lay the foundation for a healthy group. A small group should be a safe place for all who participate. Some of what will be shared is highly sensitive in nature and some may be controversial, so respect the confidentiality of the person who is sharing. Don't let your conversations leave the small group or turn into gossip. A small group is not a place to tell others what they should have done or said or think, and it's not a place to force opinions on others. Commit yourselves to listening to one another, be sensitive to their perspectives, and show them the grace you would like to receive from others.

CHAPTER ONE

The Power of "I Am"

Few of us are aware of it, but all through the day, and every day of our life, there is powerful dynamic playing out in our life that brings us success or failure. It is not about our family background, education, personality, intellect, or skills. Rather, it starts in the beliefs we have about ourselves that are then declared through the "I am"s that come out of our mouths. You know, when you're putting on your clothes and whisper, "I am so overweight," or you get caught in traffic and grump, "I am so unlucky," or you see somebody whom you think is more talented and say, "I am so average."

So what's so dynamic and powerful about something we do all the time? How are those words affecting our future? Well, here's the principle: *Whatever follows the "I am" will always come looking for you.* When you say, "I am so old," wrinkles come looking for you. When you declare, "I am always tired," fatigue is on the way. Whatever you follow the "I am" with, you're handing it an invitation, opening the door, and giving it permission to be in your life. That is a phenomenal power that we often wield against ourselves!

1. What was your immediate response to this life principle? Did you agree with it or shake your head and at least hope it's not true? Why?

   ....

   ....

2. What are the first three "I am"s that come to mind that you say on a regular basis?

   ....

   ....

   ....

   ....

David said in Psalm 139, "God, I praise You because You have made me in an amazing way. What You have done is wonderful." Notice David's "I am"s. He was saying, not in pride but in praise to God, "I am wonderful. I am amazing. I am a masterpiece." That is just as true for you. There is nothing ordinary about you. There will never be another you. You are an original. When God made you, He threw away the mold.

3. How do you feel about David's declaration about himself?

....

....

....

God made you as you are on purpose. He gave you your looks, your height, your skin color, your nose, your personality. Nothing about you is by accident. You didn't get overlooked. God calls you His masterpiece.

4. How do your thoughts about yourself line up with those thoughts?

....

....

> *Beauty is in being who God made you to be with confidence.*

....

....

....

Most of us think, *There's nothing amazing or wonderful about me. I'm just ordinary.* But we were created in the image of Almighty God.

5. Be bold and take David's declaration and write out your own, starting with your name.

....

....

....

God promised Sarai and her husband, Abram, that they would have a baby (Genesis 18). But Sarai was eighty years old, way past the child-bearing years, and in those days a childless wife was considered to be an utter failure. Imagine some of her "I am"s: "I am inferior . . . not good enough . . . worthless." God knew that the promise would never come to pass unless He could convince Sarai to change her "I am"s, so He actually changed her name from *Sarai* to *Sarah*, which means "Princess." That word got on the inside and began to change her self-image. Sarah went from believing "I am a failure" to "I am a Princess."

6. Did you ever wish you could change your name and get a new identity? Why? What would you like your new name to be?

   ....

   ....

   ....

   ....

   ....

   ....

7. Sarai had lived for a long time with a sense of shame pushing her down. Write out the things in your life that try to push you down—disappointments, bad breaks, what others have said or done to you.

   ....

   ....

   ....

   ....

   ....

   ....

Sarai allowed the spirit of a Princess to come into her and change her self-image, and she gave birth to Isaac! Start to do as she did and say, "I am royalty. I am crowned with honor. I am a child of the mighty King!"

Words have creative power. Proverbs 18:21 says, "Life and death are in the power of our tongue." It's up to you to choose what follows the "I am"s in your life. My encouragement is to never say negative things about yourself. That is cursing your future. Do yourself a favor and zip that up. Don't be against yourself.

8. Take some time now and write an honest review of the "I am"s that you say often—both positive and negative.

....

....

> *The good news is you get to choose what follows the "I am."*

....

....

....

....

....

....

....

....

....

....

In Joel 3:10 we are told, "Let the *weak* say, 'I am *strong*'"—not the opposite, "I am so powerless." That's calling in the wrong things.

9. Consider that principle about areas of your life that you want to see changed and write out three declarations "Let the _____ say, 'I am _____.'"

....

....

....

....

Romans 4 says to "call the things that are not as though they were." That simply means that you shouldn't talk about the way you are. Talk about the way you want to be. If you're struggling in your finances, don't go around saying, "Oh, man, the economy is so down. I'm never going to pay off my debt." That's calling the things that are as if they will always be that way. That's just describing the situation. By faith you have to say, "I am blessed. I am successful. I am surrounded by God's favor."

10. What was your first reaction when you read these words from Romans? Describe one specific area of your life that you will start to call it not as it is but as you want it to be.

   ....

   ....

   ....

   ....

   ....

11. Have you allowed what somebody—a coach, a teacher, a parent, an ex-spouse—said about you to hold you back? What negative seeds did they plant of what you cannot do?

   ....

   ....

   ....

   ....

   ....

> *What somebody said about you doesn't determine your destiny; God does.*

12. No matter how you feel at the moment, write out positive statements that counteract those lies based upon the fact that God has approved you.

   ....

   ....

   ....

   ....

In Numbers 13, Moses sent twelve men to spy out the Promised Land. Ten of them came back and said, "Moses, we don't have a chance. Compared to the giants we felt like grasshoppers." Notice their "I am"s. "I am weak. I am inferior. I am afraid." What happened? Fear and intimidation came knocking at the door, spreading like wildfire and infecting some 2,000,000 people with fear and inferiority.

The other two spies, Joshua and Caleb, said, "Our God is much bigger. We are well able. Let us go in and take the land at once." Their "I am"s were: "I am strong, equipped, and more than a conqueror."

13. How can you allow the right "I am"s to take root in your life. Reflect on the instructions God gave Joshua regarding his life (Joshua 1:8–9).

_____

_____

_____

_____

_____

_____

_____

14. Read these declarations out loud every day and meditate on them. As you continue to speak them, they will become a reality. Check the ones you want the most to be a part of your life.

- ❑ "I am blessed. I am prosperous. I am successful."
- ❑ "I am victorious. I am talented. I am creative."
- ❑ "I am energetic. I am happy. I am positive."
- ❑ "I am passionate. I am strong. I am confident."
- ❑ "I am secure. I am beautiful. I am attractive."
- ❑ "I am valuable. I am free. I am redeemed."
- ❑ "I am forgiven. I am anointed. I am accepted."
- ❑ "I am approved. I am prepared. I am qualified."
- ❑ "I am determined. I am patient. I am kind."
- ❑ "I am equipped. I am empowered. I am well able."
- ❑ "I am a child of the Most High God."

CHAPTER TWO

Be Positive or Be Quiet

You are where you are today in part because of what you've been saying about yourself. The Scripture says, "We will eat the fruit of our words." When you talk, you are planting seeds. When you speak something out, you give life to what you're saying. If you continue to say it, eventually that can become a reality. Whether you realize it or not, you are prophesying your future.

This is great when we're saying things such as, "I'm blessed. I will accomplish my dreams. I'm coming out of debt." That's not just being positive; you are actually prophesying victory, prophesying success, prophesying new levels. Your life will move in the direction of your words. But too many people go around prophesying just the opposite. "I never get any breaks. I'll never get back in shape. I'll probably get laid off. I always get the flu." They don't realize they are prophesying defeat.

1. How did you feel when you read the statement, "We will eat the fruit of our words"? What ways do you see this impacting your life?

   ....

   ....

   ....

   ....

   ....

   ....

2. Describe at least one statement that you make about yourself, either positive or negative, that you are reaping the fruit from on a daily basis.

   ....

   ....

   ....

Proverbs 6 states, "We are snared by the words of our mouth." *Snared* means "to be trapped." What you say can keep you from your potential and set limits for your life. You're not snared by what you think. Negative thoughts come to us all. But when you speak them out, you give them life. That's when they become a reality. When you say, "I never get any good breaks," that stops the favor that was ordained to you. If you say, "I'm not that talented. I don't have a good personality," that is calling in mediocrity. When negative thoughts come, the key is to never verbalize them. That thought will die stillborn if you don't speak it.

3. What situations or areas of your life are you facing that immediately set you back with negative thoughts?

....

....

....

....

4. Do you vent those negative thoughts, especially in the tough times? Describe whether you talk in a way that makes the problems bigger.

....

....

> *With our tongue we can bless or curse our life.*

....

....

....

5. What promise from God can help you turn this around?

....

....

....

....

God gave Jeremiah a promise that he would become a great prophet to the nations (Jeremiah 1). But when he heard God's voice, he was very young and unsure of himself. He instead listened to the other voice of doubt and defeat and said, "God, I can't do that. I can't speak to the nations. I'm too young. I wouldn't know what to say." God said, "Jeremiah, say not that you are too young."

The first thing God did was to stop his negative words. Why did God do that? Because He knew that if Jeremiah went around saying, "I'm not qualified. I can't do this. I don't have what it takes," he would become exactly what he was saying. So God said in effect, "Jeremiah, zip it up. You may think it, but don't speak it out." It goes on to tell how Jeremiah changed what he was saying, and he became a prophet to the nations.

6. Are you aware of how the voice of faith and the voice of defeat compete in specific areas of your life? Describe what the voices say.

7. Do you believe that negative words stop God's promises? How does that work out in your life?

8. Have you ever sensed God was telling you to zip the negative words? Did you zip it?

In Luke 1, when an angel appeared to a priest named Zachariah and told him that his wife was going to have a baby, he was very surprised, because he and his wife were way up there in years. He said to the angel, "Are you sure this is going to happen? It doesn't seem possible."

God knows the power of our words, and He knew that if Zachariah went around speaking defeat, it would stop His plan. So God did something unusual. He took away Zachariah's ability to speak until the baby was born. Those negative words would have stopped his destiny. That's why the Scripture says, "Put a watch over your mouth." In other words, "Be careful what you allow to come out of your mouth."

9. God has a destiny for your life as well. Do you take it seriously that your words have the power to stop or propel your destiny? In what ways?

....

....

....

....

....

....

....

....

10. Pay attention to what you are inviting into your life. Apply the promise that "I can do all things through Christ" to an area of your life in which you struggle. What are you inviting when you do that?

....

....

....

....

....

....

When God told Joshua and the people of Israel to march around the walled city of Jericho for seven straight days, He gave them one final instruction, which was the key to the whole plan working. He said, "While you march, don't say one word, not a whisper, not a short conversation, not an update on how it's going. Keep totally silent."

God knew that after a couple of times around the perimeter of the city, they would be saying, "What in the world are we doing out here? This wall is never going to fall." God knew they would talk themselves out of it. He was saying in effect, "I know you're not going to be positive, so just stay silent."

11. Have you ever felt that God asked you to do something somewhat equivalent to the people of Israel marching around the city of Jericho? Something that you wonder how it can work or help? What was it?

God knows how to bring those walls down.

12. What situation in your life do you find that it's really difficult to stay positive about? How can you pass the test and see the walls come tumbling down?

In 2 Kings 4, there is a remarkable story of a mother, her only son, and the prophet Elisha. Even though her soul was in "deep distress" from the sudden death of her son, both in verse 23, when her husband asks, and again in verse 26, when Elisha's servant asks her, she only speaks words of faith, saying, "It is well" (NKJV). Think of all the negative thoughts she was fighting, and then consider her actual words. Even in her darkest hour, when it looked impossible, she refused to speak defeat. She had a watch over her mouth and refused to be snared by her words. Remarkably, when Elisha prayed for the boy, he came back to life.

13. When people ask you about difficult situations you are facing, how do you tend to respond? Do you talk about how bad it is, or do you make a declaration of faith? Describe a response you've given in the past.

14. God resurrected this woman's son, and He has to power to resurrect dead dreams and overcome big obstacles in your life. Write down the words of faith that you will speak out loud to see God release promises that may have been delayed in your life.

CHAPTER THREE

Say So

Words have creative power. When God created the worlds, He didn't just think them into being. He didn't just believe there would be light and land and oceans and animals. He had it in His heart, but nothing happened until He spoke. He said, "Let there be light," and light came. His thoughts didn't set it into motion; His words set it into motion.

It's the same principle today. You can have faith in your heart, big dreams, be standing on God's promises, and never see anything change. What's the problem? Nothing happens until you speak. The Scripture says, "Let the redeemed of the Lord *say so*." It doesn't say, "Let the redeemed think so, or believe so, or hope so." When you speak, just like when God spoke, things begin to happen. Opportunities will find you. Good breaks, promotion, and ideas will track you down.

1. Read Genesis 1:3–29; John 1:1–4; and Hebrews 1:2; 11:3. List the action words in these verses.

   ....

   ....

   ....

   ....

2. Hope is good, but nothing happens until you speak. What are you hoping for that you need to start speaking for?

   ....

   ....

   ....

   ....

   ....

Psalm 91 says, "I will say of the Lord, 'He is my refuge, my fortress, and my shield.'" The next verse says, "He will deliver me, protect me, and cover me." Notice the connection. *I will say* and *He will do*. It doesn't say, "I believe He is my refuge. I believe He will be my strength." The psalmist went around declaring it, speaking it out: "The Lord is my refuge. The Lord is my strength." Notice what happened. God became his refuge and strength. God was saying in effect, "If you're bold enough to speak it, I'm bold enough to do it."

3. What dream has God put in your heart that has not come to pass? Have your ever declared that it is coming to pass? Write a declaration now.

Nothing happens until you speak.

---

4. You have to speak favor into your future. Write declarations of victory over your life, over your family, over your career. Start to declare them every day and believe that God will make them happen.

In the Scripture there was a lady who had been sick for many years. She had gone to the best doctors, spent all of her money trying to get well, but nothing worked. When she heard Jesus was coming through town, the Scripture says, *She kept saying to herself,* "When I get to Jesus, I know I will be made whole. Healing is on its way." In the midst of the difficulty, she was prophesying victory. When she started making her way to Jesus, it was extremely crowded, but she didn't get discouraged, and she kept saying, "This is my time." Notice the principle: Whatever you're constantly saying, you're moving toward. When she finally touched the edge of His robe, she was instantly healed.

5. Based upon your words, where are you moving toward? Are your words moving you toward health, wholeness, and breakthroughs?

6. Think for a moment about how you start your day. Write a prayer that you can say each morning that reflects God's promises and your specific needs. Make a point to declare your prayer boldly each morning.

When David faced Goliath, it looked impossible. All the odds were against him. He could have easily said, "Look, he's a giant. He's got more experience, more equipment, more talent. I can't fight him." Negative words can keep you from becoming who you were created to be. Instead, David looked Goliath in the eyes and said, "You come against me with a sword and a shield. But I come against you in the name of the Lord God of Israel. This day, I will defeat you!" Notice he was prophesying victory. He may have felt fear, but he spoke faith. He picked up that rock, slung it in his slingshot, and Goliath came tumbling down.

7. What giant are you facing? Prophesy your future and speak words of victory over it.

....

....

....

....

....

....

8. Make a list of any area of your life you want to improve in, anything you want to see changed. Then declare out loud that you are moving toward it every day.

....

Declare that your dreams are coming to pass.

....

....

....

....

....

There was a man in the Scripture name Zerubbabel. He faced a huge mountain. To rebuild the temple in Jerusalem was a big obstacle with enemies opposing every step. But he didn't talk about how impossible it was, how it was never going to work out. He said, "Who are you, oh great mountain, that would stand before me? You shall become a mere molehill." He was prophesying his future. The mountain looked big. But he declared it would be flattened out. It would become a molehill. Here's the principle: Don't talk about the mountain; talk to the mountain.

9. Read Mark 11:23. Mountains take all sorts of shapes: debt, loneliness, an addiction, a legal problem. Speak to yours and tell it, "You're coming down." Ask God to increase your faith in what He can do.

> *Prophesy what you're believing for.*

10. Describe who your Father God is, and also what it means that you are a child of the Most High God.

In the Old Testament, Ezekiel saw a vision of a valley filled with bones. It was like a huge graveyard of bones from people who had died. Bones represent things in our life that look dead, situations that seem impossible and permanently unchanging. God told him, "Ezekiel, prophesy to these dead bones. Say, 'Oh, you dry bones, hear the word of the Lord.'" As Ezekiel started speaking to the bones, telling them to come back to life, the bones started rattling and coming together, just like out of a movie, morphing back into a person. Finally, God told him to "prophesy to the breath" and call it forth. The Scripture says, "As he prophesied, breath came into those bodies, and they stood up like a vast army."

11. Do you have things in your life that seem dead—a relationship, a business, your health. God is saying to prophesy to those dead bones. Call in health. Call in abundance. Call in restoration. What do you need to call in?

12. Read these "Say So"s out loud every day and meditate on them. Check the ones you want the most to be a part of your life.

- ❏ "I will accomplish my dreams. The right people are in my future. The right opportunities are headed my way."
- ❏ "I am the head and not the tail. I will lend and not borrow."
- ❏ "My children are mighty in the land. My legacy will live on to inspire future generations."
- ❏ "I run with purpose in every step. My best days are still out in front of me. I will become everything I was created to be. I will have everything God intended for me to have. I am the redeemed of the Lord, and I *say so* today!"

CHAPTER FOUR

I Am Blessed
A Magnet for Blessings

When you honor God with your life, keeping Him in first place, He puts something on you called *a commanded blessing*. It says in Deuteronomy 28: "When you walk in God's ways, making pleasing Him your highest priority, all these blessings will chase you down and overtake you." One translation says, "You will become a magnet for blessings." The commanded blessing attracts the right people, good breaks, contracts, ideas, resources, and influence. You don't have to go after these things, trying to make something happen in your own strength or talent. All you have to do is keep honoring God and the right people and opportunities will find you. The favor, the wisdom, and the vindication will track you down. Why? You've become a magnet for God's goodness.

1. Do you feel that you are a magnet for blessings? How so?

2. What is required for you to become a magnet for God's goodness? Is anything holding you back?

When I look back over my life, it is evident that most of the favor and good breaks came to me. I didn't go after them. I was simply being my best, and God did more than I could ask or think. I spent seventeen years behind the scenes at Lakewood doing the television production. I'm not bragging, but during those seventeen years, I was faithful. I gave it my all. I wanted that broadcast to be perfect. I wasn't looking to become Lakewood's senior pastor. I was content where I was behind the scenes. But when my father went to be with the Lord, this opportunity came looking for me. I never planned on doing it; it chased me down.

3. Describe instances in your life when you sensed God's blessings upon you. Did you feel you deserved it, or was it obvious to you that the blessings were a free gift from God?

....

....

....

....

....

....

....

....

4. Describe a relationship you've had with someone whom you had to play games and try to convince them to like you. How does that contrast with a person whom God designed for you, who sees you as a treasure?

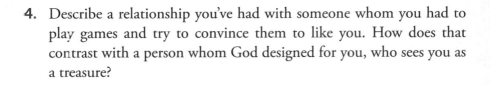

God has the right people in your future.

....

....

....

....

....

What God has planned for you is much bigger than anything you've ever dreamed. If God were to show you right now where He's taking you—the favor, the promotion, the influence—it would boggle your mind. You may not be the most qualified or talented. That's okay. God's anointing on you is more important than your talent, your education, or what family you come from. You may not see how this can happen. It doesn't seem possible. But you don't have to figure it out. If you'll just keep being your best right where you are, getting to work on time, doing more than you have to, being a person of excellence and integrity, the right people will find you and the right opportunities will track you down.

5. God said, "No good thing will I withhold because you walk uprightly." Do you realize what God is offering you in His Word? What does it mean for you to "walk uprightly"?

6. God knows the exact right time to bestow His favor upon you. How is your attitude when it doesn't happen on your timetable? What part of your character is God developing right now? How are you being faithful?

Proverbs 13 says, "The wealth of the ungodly will eventually find its way into the hands of the righteous for whom it has been laid up." Notice, because you're the righteous, there's something God has laid up for you. The good news is, at the right time, eventually it's going to find you. That means right now, favor is looking for you. Good breaks are looking for you. Healing is looking for you. Influence is looking for you. You may not have seen it yet, but don't get discouraged. Keep honoring God, and He promises some of these "eventually"s will track you down.

7. What is the difference between seeking God and seeking blessings?

....

....

....

....

8. What "eventually"s do you believe are in your future? What has your name on it and at the right time will find you?

....

....

....

....

....

....

9. Jesus said, "Seek first the kingdom and all these things will be added unto you." How does that principle apply in your life?

....

....

....

....

....

Dream big. Believe big. Pray big. Make room for God to do something new in your life. God knows what He's put in you—the gifts, the talents, the potential. You have seeds of greatness on the inside. Doors are going to open that no man can shut. Talent is going to come out of you that you didn't know you had. God is going to connect you with the right people. He will present you with opportunities that will thrust you into a new level of your destiny. Proverbs says it this way: "Trouble chases sinners, while blessings chase the righteous!"

10. God has raised you up to take new ground for the Kingdom, to go where others have not gone. What big thing are you dreaming and believing God will do in and through your life?

....

....

....

....

....

....

....

11. What seeds of greatness do you believe has God put in you—the gifts, the talents, the potential?

....

....

....

....

....

....

What if you haven't even scratched the surface of what God has in store for you?

When you realize God has put a commanded blessing on your life, and you go out each day with the attitude that something good is going to happen to you, that's when God can do the exceedingly, abundantly, above and beyond. He has explosive blessings coming your way. They are going to thrust you to a level greater than you've imagined. God knows how to get you to where you're supposed to be. All through the day, make this declaration: "I am blessed."

12. Describe two or three times when you unexpectedly saw God's favor. You didn't go after it; it came after you.

_____

_____

_____

_____

_____

_____

_____

_____

13. Write a list of the many ways you are blessed. Declare them out loud and prepare to soon step into the fullness of your destiny.

_____

_____

_____

_____

_____

_____

_____

_____

_____

CHAPTER FIVE

I Am Free
Your Seventh Year

When we've struggled in an area for a long time, it's easy to think, *This is the way it's always going to be.* Too often we see it as permanent. People tell me, "I've always been negative. That's just who I am." They've convinced themselves that it's never going to change.

The first place we lose the battle is in our own thinking. If you think it's permanent, then it's permanent. If you think you've reached your limits, you have. If you think you'll never get well, you won't. You have to change your thinking. You need to see everything that's holding you back as only temporary. It didn't come to stay; it came to pass. The moment you accept it as the norm, it can take root and become a reality. A stronghold in your mind can keep you from your destiny. If you would just break out in your thinking, you would see things begin to improve.

1. Describe an issue in your life that you've struggled with for a long time. What have you come to think about it? What do you tell yourself?

    ....

    ....

    ....

    ....

2. To break the stronghold that has taken hold in your mind, what truth will you tell yourself to stand against the lie of permanency.

    ....

    ....

    ....

    ....

In Deuteronomy 15, there was a law God gave the people of Israel that said every seventh year they had to release any Hebrew slaves. If you were Hebrew and owed someone money that you couldn't pay, they could enslave you and make you work until you paid them back. But every seventh year, if you were one of God's chosen people, no matter how much you still owed, you were set free.

This tells me God never intended His people to be permanent slaves to anything. The seventh year is when you break free from any limitation that is holding you back—sickness, addictions, debt, constant struggles. You are a child of the Most High God. You have an advantage. God promised you're not going to be a permanent slave to anything.

3. What was your immediate response to reading about this law of the seventh year? How can it impact whatever you feel is enslaving you?

....

....

....

....

....

....

4. You have to get in agreement with God and affirm, "Yes, I'm coming into my seventh year. It is my time to break free." Affirm it here by writing a declaration of what you are believing God is going to do.

....

....

....

....

....

....

God is saying, "Get ready. You are coming into your seventh year." You have to receive this into your spirit today. The seventh year is a year of release from sickness, disease, and chronic pain. Release from depression, worry, bad habits, and addictions. It's not only a release from limitations; it's a release into increase. God is about to release you into new opportunities, good breaks, and new levels. He is going to release ideas, creativity, sales, contracts, and business. The seventh year is when you get released into overflow, into more than enough. It's when dreams come to pass because things have shifted in your favor.

5. Focus your thoughts beyond a release from limitations and on to a release into increase. What do you want to see God release into your life that will bring you into overflow, where your dreams come to pass?

It's going to be bigger, better, and more rewarding than you thought possible.

6. When you believe, all things are possible. Dare to write and thank God for the release of more than enough that is coming in your seventh year.

When you're in tough times, and it looks as though you're never going to break out, do as Moses did. The Israelites had been in slavery for hundreds of years. It looked permanent. Moses had a son, whom he named *Gershom*, which means, "I am an alien in a strange land." When Moses named his son, he was making a declaration of faith. He was saying, "We're in slavery, but slavery is not our norm. This is not our permanent address. We are foreigners in this land." Every time he said, "Good morning, Gershom," he was reminding himself, "This lack, this trouble, this slavery, is not our normal state. We will be free."

7. God can turn any situation around. He has you in the palm of His hand and is bringing you into your seventh year. To get ready for your seventh years, how can you begin to talk and act as if it's going to happen?

   ....

   ....

   ....

   ....

   ....

8. The Apostle Paul described life's tough times this way: "These light afflictions are for a moment." In your mind, what you are facing may be big, but by faith write a declaration that it is only light and temporary.

   ....

   ....

   ....

   ....

   ....

   ....

   ....

In the Scripture, King Hezekiah was very sick and had been told by the prophet Isaiah that he was going to die. It looked permanent, as though his days were over. Hezekiah could have accepted it and thought, *It's my lot in life*. But Hezekiah had a boldness. He chose to believe even when it looked impossible. The Scripture says, "He turned his face to the wall and started praying." Before Isaiah could leave the palace grounds, God spoke to him and said, "Go back and tell Hezekiah that I'm going to give him fifteen more years." Here's what I want you to see. Hezekiah's faith brought about his seventh year. Faith is what causes God to move.

9. When we take our problems to God, we often stop there and make it into a complaining session. How would you describe your prayer life when you approach God with your problems?

....

....

....

....

10. Hezekiah didn't complain or wait for his health to turn around before he gave God praise. Praise activates God's favor. Have the boldness of Hezekiah and write a prayer of praise that elevates you beyond the problem and exalts God as your Jehovah Jireh; the Lord your Provider.

....

....

....

....

....

....

....

....

....

Isaiah said, "The Spirit of the Lord is upon me to announce freedom to the captives." He was saying in effect, "It may look permanent, but I'm announcing your freedom—from whatever enslaves you—and new levels in your future." Then Isaiah took it one step further. "I'm declaring the Year of God's Favor." He announced it, then he declared it.

What if we would do the same thing? "I'm announcing today we're coming out of debt, struggle, and not getting ahead. I'm declaring we're coming into increase, overflow, and abundance." Or, "I'm announcing, 'We will not live negative, depressed, worried, anxious, or stressed out.' I'm declaring, 'We are happy, content, confident, secure, full of joy, and loving our lives.'" You have to announce it and declare it by faith.

11. You are coming into your seventh year. I believe and declare that every limitation has been broken. God is releasing you into increase, opportunity, favor, healing, and breakthroughs. Now is your time. Write out your announcement here and declare it by faith.

"I am free. I am healthy. I am blessed. God's favor is coming—breakthroughs, healing, and promotions are on the way."

CHAPTER SIX

I Am Valuable
Know Who You Are

When God created you in His image, He put a part of Himself in you. You could say that you have the DNA of Almighty God. You are destined to do great things, destined to leave your mark on this generation. Your Heavenly Father spoke worlds into existence. He flung stars into space. He designed every flower. He made man out of dust and breathed life into him. Now here's the key. He is not just the Creator of the universe. He is not just the all-powerful God. He is your Heavenly Father. You have His DNA. Imagine what you can do.

But too many times we focus on our weaknesses and mistakes, what we don't have, and the family we come from. We end up settling for mediocrity when we were created for greatness. If you're going to break out of average, you need to remind yourself of who you are.

1. Write an honest review of who you think you are—not who you wish you were, but what your real thoughts are when you look in the mirror.

When you know who you are, you'll start thinking, talking, and carrying yourself like you are a winner.

When you gave your life to Christ, the Scripture talks about how you became a new creation. You were born into a new family. You entered into a new royal bloodline. You are God's child. You have His spiritual DNA. So don't you dare go around thinking that you're average. Your Father created worlds. There's nothing too much for you. You can overcome that sickness. You can run that company. You can take your family to a new level. Quit believing the lies that say, "You've reached your limits." Start talking to yourself as a winner. It's in your blood.

2. If you read a billboard that asked, "Who is your Heavenly Father?" how would you describe Him?

....

....

....

....

....

....

....

....

3. Based upon your spiritual DNA, what are you capable of doing or being that you need talk to yourself as a winner?

....

....

....

....

....

....

....

....

....

If you look back and study your spiritual bloodline in the family of God, you'll see your ancestor Moses parted the Red Sea. There's great faith in your bloodline. David, a shepherd boy, defeated a giant. There's favor in your bloodline. Nehemiah rebuilt the walls of Jerusalem when all the odds were against him. There's increase, promotion, and abundance in your bloodline. A young lady named Esther stepped up and saved her people from a certain death. There is courage in your bloodline.

When thoughts tell you that it's never going to happen, just check your spiritual birth certificate. Remind yourself of who you are.

4. What biblical person do you most desire to be like? Why? What's holding you back?

> *You were born to win, born to overcome, born to live in victory.*

5. It says in the Psalms, "God's favor surrounds me like a shield," because of who we are. Do your thoughts tell you otherwise? Write a statement about who you are that defeats that thought.

Maybe nobody has told you who you are. Almighty God says:

- You're a child of the Most High God.
- You are strong. You are talented.
- You are beautiful. You are wise.
- You are courageous. You have seeds of greatness.
- You can do all things through Christ.
- You didn't come from ordinary stock.
- You're a thoroughbred. You have winning in your DNA.
- You are destined to do great things.

6. What did you immediately feel when you read those statements? In what ways do they align with your thoughts about yourself?

....

....

....

....

....

....

7. In Luke 13, when Jesus saw a woman who had been bent over with a sickness for eighteen years, He said, "Should not this woman be loosed from this sickness seeing that she is a daughter of Abraham?" If He was standing before you today, what would He would say about you?

....

....

....

....

....

....

....

....

In Judges 6, an angel appeared to a man named Gideon, who was hiding in the fields after a powerful nation had overtaken the people of Israel, and said, "Mighty hero, the Lord is with you." Gideon felt that he was just the opposite—he was the least, inadequate, and not able to deliver his people. It seemed that he was just another ordinary, insignificant man. But God saw something in Gideon that other people did not see. God saw his potential. God saw what he could become.

Gideon didn't know who he was, and the same is often true for us. Turn off the negative recording that's reminding you of what you're not, and get in agreement with God. Start seeing yourself as that mighty hero.

8. If an angel came looking for you to be a mighty hero and accomplish something great, how would you respond?

....

....

....

....

....

....

....

9. What potential do you think God sees in you that others don't see?

....

....

....

....

....

....

....

Toward the end of this book chapter, I told the story about the eagle that was born and raised in a chicken coop. For years he acted like a chicken because that's all he'd ever seen. But one day he saw a soaring eagle and realized who he really was. Perhaps you've come from a very limited environment and that's how you feel as well. Draw a line in the sand and say, "I'm not settling here. I know who I am. I am an eagle. I am a king's son. I am a mighty hero. I have winning in my DNA."

10. Despite Moses being raised and trained in Pharaoh's court, when God told him to go tell Pharaoh to let the people go, the first thing Moses said was, "Who am I?" He forgot who he was. What excuses do you make when God tells you what He wants you to do?

-----

11. Perhaps you're an eagle that has been in a chicken coop way too long. What line do you need to draw in the sand, and what is that you need to declare to become everything God has created you to be?

CHAPTER SEVEN

I Am a Masterpiece
See Yourself as a Masterpiece

Ephesians 2:10 says, "We are God's masterpiece." When God created you, He went to great lengths to make you exactly as He wanted. You didn't accidentally get your personality. You didn't just happen to get your height, your looks, your skin color, or your gifts. There will never be another you. God designed you on purpose to be the way you are. You have what you need to fulfill your destiny. If you're going to reach your highest potential, you have to see yourself as unique, as an original, as God's very own masterpiece.

1. How do you see yourself right now in the light of Ephesians 2:10?

   ....

   ....

   ....

   ....

   ....

2. What can you do to be more confident in who God made you to be?

   ....

   ....

   ....

   ....

   ....

   ....

You are God's most prized possession. You've been painted by the most incredible Painter there could ever be. When God created you, He stepped back and looked and said, "You're amazing. You're wonderful. Another masterpiece!" He stamped His approval on you.

Our value doesn't come because of what we look like, or what we do, or who we know. Our value comes from the fact that Almighty God is our Painter. So don't criticize what God has painted. Quit wishing you were taller, or had a different personality, or looked like somebody else. You have been fearfully and wonderfully made. Accept yourself. Approve yourself. Get in agreement with what God says about you.

3. What are the things about yourself that you don't feel good about . . . the things that you put yourself down about?

Life will try to push you down and steal your sense of value.

4. Write a declaration that you have the fingerprints of God all over you— the way you look, the way you smile, your gifts, your personality.

Jesus said to love your neighbor as you love yourself. If you don't love yourself in a healthy way, you will never be able to love others in the way that you should. This is why some people don't have good relationships. If you don't get along with yourself, you'll never get along with others. We all have weaknesses, shortcomings, things that we wish were different. But God never designed us to go through life being against our self. The opinion you have of yourself is the most important opinion that you have. If you see yourself as less than, not talented, not valuable, you will convey those feelings, and people will treat you inferior. If you are proud of who God made you to be, people will see you as strong, talented, and valuable and treat you accordingly.

5. Describe the areas where you have problems in relationships. Is it related to whether you love yourself in a healthy way?

....

....

....

....

....

....

....

6. What messages do you think you are sending out about yourself? What can you change about your own opinion of yourself that will send new messages that lead to new opportunities and relationships?

....

....

....

....

....

....

....

The Scripture talks about how God has made us to be kings and priests unto Him. Start carrying yourself as royalty. Not in arrogance, thinking that you're better than others, but in humility be proud of who God made you to be. You are not better than anyone else, but you are not less than anyone else. Understand, your Father created the whole universe. When He breathed His life into you and sent you to planet earth, you didn't come as ordinary. You didn't come as average. You are crowned not by people but by Almighty God. Now start thinking as royalty, talking as royalty, dressing as royalty, walking as royalty, and acting as royalty.

7. How do you react to the thought that God has made you to be a king or queen? How does that make you feel in relationship to others?

You don't have to do enough good and then maybe God will crown you. He already has.

8. If you start to think as royalty, how will it change the way you live— the way you talk, dress, walk, and act? How will you wear your crown?

When Jesus was being baptized by John in the Jordan River, He had not performed a single miracle or spoken to any great crowds. But a voice boomed out of the heavens, and God said, "This is My beloved Son in whom I am well pleased." His Father was pleased with Him because of who He was and not because of anything He had or had not done.

You may think, *That's not me. I've got a lot of flaws.* Get out of that defeated mentality. You may not be perfect, but God is not basing your value on your performance. He's looking at whether you have a heart to please Him. Now quit being down on yourself. Quit living condemned and dare to believe God has already approved you.

9. How can you learn to accept yourself while you're in the process of changing?

   ....

   ....

   ....

   ....

   ....

10. If you don't like yourself, you will never become who God created you to be. What are you against in yourself that is holding you back?

    ....

    ....

    ....

    ....

    ....

    ....

    ....

    ....

    ....

In Genesis 1, God had just created the heavens, the earth, the animals, and Adam and Eve. When He finished, the Scripture says, "God looked over all that He had made and saw how it was excellent in every way." When God looks at you, He says, "You are excellent in every way."

God breathed His life into you. Get up every morning and remind yourself that your value comes because of whose you are. Be bold enough to celebrate who God made you to be. Be proud of who you are. Dare to say as David declared, "I am amazing. I am talented. I am one of a kind. I am a masterpiece."

11. What is your comfort level when you read that you need to celebrate who God made you to be? What are your immediate thoughts?

....

....

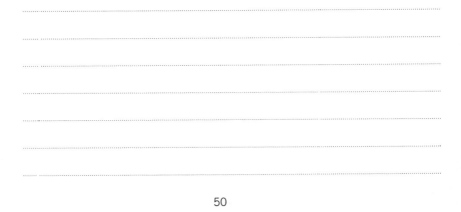

Maybe you need to change the recording that's playing in your mind.

....

....

....

....

....

12. Write a statement of faith declaring you are God's masterpiece, then copy it on another sheet of paper and place it on your bathroom mirror and repeat it out loud every morning.

....

....

....

....

....

....

....

....

CHAPTER EIGHT

I Am Content
Living Content

It's good to have dreams and goals. We should be stretching our faith, believing for something bigger. But while we're waiting for things to change, waiting for promises to come to pass, we shouldn't be discontent where we are. When we're unhappy, frustrated, and discontent, we're dishonoring God. We're so focused on what we want that we're taking for granted what we have.

The Apostle Paul said, "I have learned how to be content, whether I'm abased or abounding, whether I have plenty or whether I'm in need." Notice he had to *learn* to be content. It doesn't happen automatically. It's a choice we have to make. Being content doesn't mean that we don't want change, give up on our dreams, or settle where we are. It means we're not frustrated. We know God is working behind the scenes, and at the right time He will get us to where we're supposed to be.

1. On a scale of 1 to 10, with 1 being frustrated and discontent and 10 being content, how would you grade yourself? Describe where you are at.

Being unhappy with a situation is not going to make it happen any sooner.

I've found some situations will not change until we change. As long as we're frustrated, stressed out, and discontent about our job or the kids or the size of our house, that's going to keep us where we are. God's plan for our life is not to just make us comfortable but to grow us up, to mature us, so He can release more of His favor. We may not like where we are, but we wouldn't be there unless God had a purpose for it. God is going to use it to do a work in us. When we're content, we're growing. We're developing character. Our faith is being strengthened. You could easily complain, but you say, "Lord, thank You for this." That's passing the test. Instead of trying to change the situation, let it change you.

2. Paul had to learn to be content, so we're in good company. What areas of your life do you find the hardest in which to be content?

3. What do you believe God is trying to work in your life through these tests?

David spent *years* in the lonely shepherd's fields taking care of his father's sheep . . . *after* he had been chosen to be the next king of Israel. The prophet Samuel had already anointed him. David could have thought, *God, this isn't right. I've got big dreams. You promised me great things. What am I doing stuck out here with a bunch of sheep?*

But David understood this principle. He didn't live stressed or frustrated. He knew that God was in control, so he just kept being his best, going to work with a good attitude, grateful for where he was. Because he was content in the shepherd's fields, he made it to the throne, to the palace. As Paul did, he learned to be content and passed that test.

4. Describe a situation in which you learned to be content. What was the positive result that it yielded?

....

....

....

....

....

....

Unresolved discontentment will follow you everywhere you go.

5. If you have a dream that is not coming to pass, that's a test. How can you do as David did and bloom where you're planted?

....

....

....

....

....

....

....

....

Think about Mary, the mother of Christ. When she was late in her pregnancy with Jesus, she had to ride a donkey to Bethlehem and then give birth in a barn. She could have complained, "God, if I'm going to have this baby for You, at least You could make it more comfortable for me." However, Mary was content when the angel said, "You've been highly favored," and content riding a donkey while pregnant, content giving birth in a barn with a bunch of animals, and content when the wise men said, "Your son is the Messiah." It takes a mature person to be content on the mountaintop and content in the valley.

6. How much of your contentment is based on what you have or don't have, on who likes you or who doesn't like you?

   ....

   ....

   ....

   ....

7. Scripture says, "Godliness with contentment is great gain." What did the Apostle Paul mean by that?

   ....

   ....

   ....

   ....

   ....

8. You may have a thousand reasons to live unhappy, but write a declaration that you have made the choice to be content.

   ....

   ....

   ....

   ....

   ....

Life is full of seasons. There has to be planting seasons, watering seasons, and maintaining seasons. Without going through that process, you're not going to come into a harvest season. Instead of being frustrated by this season's difficulties, realize it is getting you prepared for promotion. God has given you the grace you need not in order to endure this season—that doesn't take any faith—but to enjoy the season.

You may be in one of those difficult seasons right now, raising a small child, taking care of an elderly loved one, or perhaps dealing with an illness. It's easy to think, *As soon as I get through this tough time, I'll get my joy back.* No, this is the day the Lord has made. When you're content, you see each day as a gift. You have to choose to rejoice today.

9. Describe the season you are in. What challenges has it brought to you that are making you stronger and developing your character?

....

....

....

....

....

....

....

10. During this season, what has God given you to be grateful for?

....

....

....

....

....

....

....

....

A mistake we make too often is that we think that when we reach a certain goal, then we'll be happy. "As soon as . . . , I'll enjoy my life." Yes, you'll be happy when you accomplish your goals, but there are challenges that come along with it. You'll never come to a place where you're problem-free, having no conflicts and no bills to pay, and everybody is celebrating you. That's not reality. If you don't learn to be content where you are, you won't be content when your dreams come to pass. And because you're waiting for things to change, you're missing the beauty of this moment, the joy of today. Don't go through life always wanting something else. See the gift in what you have right now.

11. The real joy in life is in the simple things, such as playing hide-and-seek with our kids or watching the sunset with our spouse. List ten simple things that you can find pleasure in today.

12. How can you embrace the place where you are, see the good, and be grateful for what you have?

CHAPTER NINE

I Am Secure

Be Comfortable with Who You Are

There is an underlying pressure in our society to be number one. If we're not the best, the leader, the fastest, the most talented, the most beautiful, or the most successful, we're taught to not feel good about ourselves. We have to work harder. We have to run faster. We must stay ahead.

One of the best things I've ever learned is to be comfortable with who God made me to be. I believe God has given me a specific assignment in life and gifted me with exactly what I need for the race that's been designed for me. I don't have to outperform anyone to feel good about myself. I don't have to out build, outdrive, outrace, out minister, or outproduce anyone. It's not about anyone else. It's about becoming who God made me to be.

1. Describe the pressures you feel and have felt to excel and get ahead and climb the ladder. How have you responded to that pressure?

> *There will always be somebody more successful, more talented, and more beautiful.*

I'm all for having goals, stretching, and believing big. That's important. But you have to accept the gift that God has given you. You shouldn't feel less than if someone seems to have a more significant gift. God has given you a gift that's unique, something that will propel you into your destiny and cause you to leave your mark on this generation.

Here's the key. You don't have to have a great gift for God to use it in a great way. Do you know what gift put David on the throne? It wasn't his leadership skills, his dynamic personality, or his ability to write and play music. It was his gift to sling a rock. That seemingly insignificant gift enabled him to defeat Goliath and eventually put David on the throne. Never discount any gift that God has given you.

2. What gift/gifts do you believe God has given you? What do you base that belief upon? What would you say makes you tick?

_____

_____

_____

_____

_____

_____

_____

_____

3. In what ways have you discounted your gifts in the past . . . and today?

_____

_____

_____

_____

_____

_____

_____

Too often we pursue titles and positions, thinking we'll feel good about ourselves when we have them. Titles are fine, but you don't need a title to do what God has called you to do. Don't wait for people to approve you, affirm you, or validate you. Use your gift, and the title will come.

When David went out to face Goliath, his title was shepherd. People told him he was not qualified, too small, and would get hurt. What David had, and what you have, may seem small. You may feel intimidated and unqualified. That's okay. It didn't stop David. If you'll use what you have, God will breathe on it. His anointing on that simple gift will cause you to step into the fullness of your destiny.

4. Write an honest review of whether you are following your dreams or stuck in a pursuit of a title or position.

> *You can't wait for people's approval to do what God has called you to do.*

5. How can you start today to more fully do what God has put in your heart and use your gift in whatever way you can?

In the Scripture there was a little boy. All he had was a sack lunch—five loaves of bread, two fish. Nothing much. Not very significant. Yet, when thousands of people were hungry, Jesus took his lunch, multiplied it, and fed the whole crowd. We hear a lot about the little boy being willing to give the lunch, but who was more important—the little boy with the lunch or the mother who made the lunch? Without the mother, we wouldn't be talking about the miracle. She used her gift that seemed small to make a lunch that is world renown. Her assignment and gifts were different than Queen Esther, whose courage saved her nation, but she was not competing with Esther. She was being faithful with her gift.

6. To what level would you say you are secure enough to play the role that God has given you in life?

In this book chapter, I stated: "I realize there are some positions that carry more weight and more importance, but in God's eyes the usher is just as important as the pastor. They're just running different races."

7. What was your first reaction to that statement?

A lot of times we think, *If I had their talent and looks and career, I'd be happy.* But the truth is that if you traded places, you wouldn't be fulfilled, because their gifts, talents, skills, and personality have been uniquely designed for their assignment. You could try to do what they're doing, but the problem is the anointing on your life is for your gifts, for what you're called to do. If you just be the best that you can be with what you have, there will be a fulfillment, a satisfaction. God will open up doors. He will get you to where you're supposed to be. When you're comfortable with who you are, walking in your anointing, you enjoy life.

8. Competing with others is a frustrating way to live. In what ways do you find yourself caught up in competing and comparing with others?

    ....

    ....

    ....

    ....

    ....

9. What results do you get from trying to outperform and impress others?

    ....

    ....

    ....

    ....

    ....

    ....

10. How can you break out of that and start running your own race?

    ....

    ....

    ....

    ....

    ....

    ....

King Saul had been happy running his own race. Life was good until he heard some women saying, "Saul has killed thousands, and David has killed tens of thousands." From that moment on, he never looked at David the same way. What was his problem? He couldn't handle somebody getting ahead of him. He spent months and months trying to kill David, all because he wasn't comfortable with who he was.

Can you celebrate people who pass you by? Can you be happy for them and stay focused on your own race? Our attitude should be, *I may not be at that person's level, but I'm going to be the best person you've ever seen. I'm going to become all God has created me to be.*

11. This is where the rubber really meets the road. How happy are you for people who pass you by?

12. What can you do to improve your attitude so that you can celebrate others' achievements as well as your own?

If you learn to comfortable with who you are, you'll not only enjoy your life more, but you will rise higher, your gifts and talents will come out to the full, and you will become everything that God has created you to be!

CHAPTER TEN

I Am Victorious
It's under Your Feet

How we see our difficulties very often will determine whether or not we get out of them. When things mount against us, it's easy to start thinking, *This is never going to work out. I'll just have to learn to live with it.* But 1 Corinthians 15 talks about how God has put all things under our feet. If you're going to live in victory, you have to see every sickness, every obstacle, and every temptation as being under your feet. It's no match for you. It's just a matter of time before you walk it out.

This is what David did. He faced all kinds of enemies. He said in Psalm 59, "I will look down in triumph on *all* of my enemies." Notice that David said "*all* of my enemies." So what am I going to do with difficulties—the financial debt, the addiction, the weight problem? Look down. Why? Because they're all under my feet.

1. Review your response to a recent difficulty that you faced. To what degree did you look down on it or look up at it? How might you improve your response in the future?

> *If you want to say something to the enemy, write it on the bottom of your shoe.*

God stated, "I have given you power to tread on all the power of the enemy." Think of that word *tread*. One translation says "to trample." You are not weak, defeated, or inferior. You are full of "can do" power. The same Spirit that raised Christ from the dead lives on the inside of you. Now start putting obstacles and difficulties under your feet.

The Scripture says, "The joy of the Lord is your strength." Joy is an emotion, and yet it creates strength. When you're in tough times, you have to shake off the worry, the self-pity, the disappointment. Get your joy back. Have the right perspective. That sickness, that obstacle—it's under your feet. It's not going to defeat you. It's going to promote you.

2. What was your immediate response to the statement that God has given you power to tread or trample on all the power of the enemy? In what ways have you experienced this power?

_____

_____

_____

_____

_____

_____

3. What role does the joy of the Lord have in your daily life? How can you make it more of a strength to counteract tough times?

_____

_____

_____

_____

_____

_____

_____

_____

In 2 Samuel 22, it says, "You have armed me with strength for the battle. You have put my enemies under my feet." God knows every battle that you will ever face, including every temptation and every obstacle. He has not only put it under your feet, but He has armed you with strength for that battle. He has already equipped you. Quit telling yourself, "This is too much. I can't handle it." The greatest force in the universe is breathing in your direction. Tap into that power. Start declaring, "This is under my feet. God is in control. I am well able. I can do all things through Christ. I am strong in the Lord."

4. Do you think the enemy considers you "Armed and Dangerous"? How so?

....

....

....

....

5. Write a statement of faith that you can use to declare first thing in the morning to power up for a blessed, victorious, faith-filled day.

....

....

....

....

....

....

....

....

....

....

....

Psalm 110 says, "God will make your enemies your footstool." What do you do with a footstool? You put your feet up on it and rest. When we face difficulties, too often we take matters into our own hands. We think, *They did me wrong. I'm going to pay them back.* Or our medical report is not good, and we're so uptight we can't sleep at night. But if you want God to make your enemy your footstool, you have to be still and know that He is God. When you're living upset and trying to force things to happen, God is going to let you try to do it on your own. It takes faith to say, "God, I know You are fighting my battles. You promised it would work out for my good. So I'm going to keep my joy and stay in peace."

6. What difficulty are facing today that you need to put your feet up and rest, so to speak, and let God make into your footstool?

....

....

....

....

7. What truths about God will help you to stay in peace and keep your joy when you're feeling upset, anxious, and panicked?

....

....

....

....

When you stay in peace, God will take what's meant for harm and use it to your advantage.

....

....

....

....

....

....

All the things that come against us to try to get us upset—people talking, gossiping, spreading rumors, not giving us respect—are all distractions. That's the enemy trying to lure us off course, get us bent out of shape, and waste valuable time and energy on something that doesn't really matter. Don't give that the time of day. That's not a battle you're supposed to fight. David said in Psalm 23: "God will prepare a table before you in the presence of your enemies." That means God will not only make your wrongs right, but God will bless you in front of your enemies. He will give you honor, recognition, and favor in front of the people who tried to pull you down. Stay in peace. God has you covered!

8. Describe a situation where you were the target of people's gossip and rumors and disrespect.

_____

_____

_____

_____

_____

_____

_____

9. In that situation, did you stay in peace, believing that God had your back? How would you improve on your response if it comes up again?

_____

_____

_____

_____

_____

_____

_____

_____

_____

The prophet Isaiah said, "No weapon formed against you will prosper." It doesn't say that we won't have difficulties or ever have a problem. That's not reality. It says, "People may talk. You may get a negative medical report. A family member may get off course. The problem may form, but you can stay in peace, knowing that it's not going to prosper against you." Because you're His child, because you're in the secret place of the Most High, God has a hedge of protection, mercy, and favor around you that the enemy cannot cross. No person, no sickness, and no trouble can stop God's plan for your life or keep you from your destiny.

10. Name a problem that is presently formed against you. How does the perspective that the problem is not going to prosper impact you today?

....

....

....

....

....

....

....

....

11. In what ways have you seen God's hedge of protection, mercy, and favor around your life?

....

....

....

....

....

....

....

CHAPTER ELEVEN

I Am Prosperous
Have an Abundant Mentality

God's dream for your life is that you would be blessed in such a way that you could be a blessing to others. David said, "My cup runs over." God is an overflow God. He is called El Shaddai, the God of More Than Enough. Not the God of Barely Enough or the God of Just Help Me Make It Through. He's the God of Abundance.

Psalm 35 says, "Let them say continually, 'Let the Lord be magnified who takes pleasure in the prosperity of His children.'" They were supposed to go around constantly saying, "God takes pleasure in prospering me." It was to help them develop this abundant mentality. Your life is moving toward what you're constantly thinking about. If you're always thinking thoughts of lack, not enough, and struggle, you're moving toward the wrong things. All through the day, meditate on these thoughts: overflow, abundance. God takes pleasure in prospering you.

1. What was your first reaction to the statement from Psalm 35? What do you feel about the name El Shaddai, the God of More Than Enough?

....

....

....

....

| *He's the God of Overflow.* |

....

....

....

The Scripture says God will supply our needs "according to His riches." So often we look at our situations and think, *I'll never get ahead. I'll never get out.* But it's not according to what you have; it's according to what He has. The good news is God owns it all. One touch of God's favor can blast you out of Barely Enough and put you into More Than Enough. God has ways to increase you beyond your normal income and what's predictable. Quit telling yourself, "This is all I'll ever have." Let go of that and have an abundant mentality. "I'm not staying here. I am blessed and prosperous. I am headed to the land of More Than Enough."

2. God took the Israelites from the land of Barely Enough and slavery to the land of Just Enough in the wilderness to the land of More Than Enough in the Promised Land. Where is He taking you?

3. How will you keep from putting your stakes down in the land of Barely Enough and the land of Just Enough?

Jesus told a parable about a prodigal son. This young man left home and blew all of his money, wasted his inheritance, and decided to return home. When his father saw him—the father represents God—he said to the staff, "Go kill the fatted calf. We're going to have a party." But the older brother got upset. He said, "Dad, I've been with you this whole time, and you've never even given me a skinny goat."

You can survive in the land of Barely Enough to make it through. You can endure in the land of Just Enough to pay the bills. But that is not God's best. Your Heavenly Father is saying, "I have a fatted calf for you. I have a place for you in the land of More Than Enough."

4. Do you have a fatted calf or a skinny goat mentality? Explain.

    ....

    ....

    ....

    ....

    ....

5. God wants you to overflow with His goodness. How does your thinking need to change to get to abundance in all areas of your life?

    ....

    ....

    ....

    ....

    ....

6. One touch of God's favor can thrust you into more than enough. Talk yourself into it by declaring your faith in His character and name today.

    ....

    ....

    ....

    ....

    ....

Jesus talked about how when we give, it will be given back to us as good measure, pressed down, shaken together, and running over. He is saying that He will take what you give, press it down, and make room for more of His increase and show you His favor in a new way. After He presses it down, He is going to shake it together and not just fill it to the top. He is going to take it one step farther and give you so much that you're running over. That's the way our God is.

7. If you keep being faithful right where you are, honoring God in all your giving, what do you expect God will do?

> *God says, "I am bringing you out of lack into a good and spacious land."*

8. The Scripture asks us, "Is there anything too hard for the Lord?" What do you need that you have felt was just too much to expect from God?

Why don't you get in agreement and say, "God, I'm ready. I'm a giver. I have an abundant mentality. Lord, I want to thank You for good measure, pressed down, shaken together, and running over in my life."

In *The Message* translation, Deuteronomy 28 states, "God will lavish you with good things. He will throw open the doors of His sky vaults and rain down favor. You will always be the top dog and never the bottom dog."

9. If you were to see yourself as the top dog, what would you look like?

    ....

    ....

    ....

10. Write a statement of faith that gives God the permission to lavish you with good things.

    ....

    ....

    ....

    ....

    ....

11. The Scripture says, "It is the Lord who gives you power to get wealth." If God gives you power to get wealth, why do some people feel that it is wrong to state that and to have wealth?

    ....

    ....

    ....

    ....

    ....

12. Money is simply a tool to accomplish your destiny and to advance His Kingdom. How can you make sure it remains just that?

    ....

    ....

    ....

    ....

My prayer for you is found in Deuteronomy 1:11. It says, "May the Lord God of your fathers increase you a thousand times more than you are." Can you receive that into your spirit? A thousand times more favor. A thousand times more resources. A thousand times more income. Most of the time our thinking goes *TILT! TILT! TILT!* It's because we've been hanging out with that skinny goat too long. It's time to cut him loose. It's time to have a fatted calf mentality. I believe and declare you won't live in the land of Just Enough or the land of Barely Enough, but you're coming into the land of More Than Enough.

13. You are not going to bankrupt Heaven by believing for an abundant life. What big dreams do you have in your heart? Not just for yourself, but to help others. It's okay if your thinking goes *TILT!*

Get up every morning and say, "Lord, I want to thank You that You are opening up Your sky vaults today, raining down favor, and lavishing me with good things. I am prosperous."

CHAPTER TWELVE

I Am Focused
Redeem the Time

Time is more valuable than money. You can make more money, but you can't make more time. The Scripture tells us to redeem the time and use it wisely. That means, don't waste it. Don't live this day unfocused, undisciplined, and unmotivated. This day and this life is a gift. Are you living it to the full? With purpose and passion? Pursuing your dreams? Or are you distracted? Indifferent? Just doing whatever comes along? Are you in a job you don't like? Hanging out with people who are pulling you down? That's not redeeming the time; that's wasting the time. You're either investing your life or you're wasting it.

1. Do you have an intentional, strategic plan for what you want to do with your life and what you want be? Write it here.

Is it a plan with set goals, or is it actually your hopes? Hope is not a plan.

Many people are talented and have great potential, but they're not disciplined with how they spend their time. Paul said in Ephesians, "Make the most of every opportunity. Don't be vague and thoughtless, but live purposefully and accurately." If you're going to reach your highest potential, you have to be an "on purpose" person. You know where you're going, are focused on a plan, organized, and taking action. You're not vague, distracted, waiting to see what happens.

2. While entertainment has its place, it typically consumes great chunks of our time. Review how much time you give to social media, video games, television, sports, movies, the Internet, etc.

3. The Scripture talks about living well spent lives. What specific steps will you take to improve your use of time and taking steps toward your goals and becoming who God's created you to be?

On a regular basis, you need to reevaluate what you're doing. Refocus your life. Get rid of any distractions. Paul said, "I run with purpose in every step." When we understand the value of time and see each day as the gift that it is, it helps us to keep the right perspective. You don't waste your valuable time fighting battles that don't matter—the conflicts that are not between you and your God-given destiny. If somebody has a problem with you, as long as you're being your best, doing what God's put in your heart, with all due respect, that's their problem and not yours. It is not your responsibility to make them happy or win their approval.

4. Write an honest review of how much time you spend fighting battles that don't matter—answering critics, seeking others' approval, etc.

....

....

....

....

....

....

....

....

> *Do you have to resolve conflicts with every person?*

5. What is it that you tell yourself that opens the door to fighting battles that are not worth fighting? How can you stop the trigger?

....

....

....

....

....

....

....

....

The Scripture says, "Don't let the sun go down on your anger." The reason many people have no joy or enthusiasm is because they live with unforgiveness in their heart. They spend lots of time reliving their hurts, thinking about their disappointments. Here's the problem: If the sun goes down with bitterness and resentment, it will come back up with bitterness and resentment. That blocks God's blessings. It keeps you from seeing a bright future as well as from investing your time wisely.

6. Are you living with unforgiveness, worries, disappointments, and hurts? Write down what they are and a statement that you are releasing them to God.

....

....

....

....

....

....

....

....

When you feel your life is stuck in a rut, invest your time wisely in helping others. Those seeds that you sow will create a harvest not to just get you out of the valley but to come to a new level of your destiny.

7. How can you invest your time in other people's lives and bless them?

....

....

....

....

....

It's not only important how we spend our time, but with whom we spend it. The only thing that's keeping some people from a new level of their destiny is wrong friendships. To redeem the time may mean you have to prune some relationships that are not adding value to your life. Don't hang around people who are not going anywhere, who have no goals or dreams. If you hang out with jealous, critical, unhappy people, you will end up jealous, critical, and unhappy. That's what it says in Proverbs: When you walk with wise men, you will become wise.

8. Consider the character qualities of your friends in the light of your desire to become who God created you to be. Do they have the integrity and spirit of excellence that will lift you up rather than drag you down?

> *You cannot hang out with chickens and expect to soar like an eagle.*

9. If you don't let go of the wrong people, you'll never meet the right people. Who do you need to let go of or spend less time with?

When Jesus was on the earth, He was very selective with His friendships. Everyone wanted to be close to Him. But He chose only twelve disciples with whom to spend most of His highly valuable time. Out of those twelve, three were his close friends: Peter, James, and John. One could be considered his best friend, John. He was described as the disciple whom Jesus loved. You have to be careful who you allow in your inner circle. You may have twenty people you call friends, but make sure the two or three you choose to be close to you believe in you, stick up for you, and are with you through thick or thin. Invest your time wisely.

10. Who makes up the inner circle of your life? Should they be there?

11. In Mark 5, when Jesus prayed for a little girl who had died, He put out of the room the people who didn't believe in Him and would drag Him down. Is there someone in your inner circle whom you need to let go of and simply love from a distance?

CHAPTER THIRTEEN

I Am Determined
Finishing Grace

It doesn't take a lot of effort to start things—a diet, school, a family. Starting is easy. Finishing is what can be difficult. Anyone can have a dream, but it takes determination, perseverance, and a made-up mind to see it come to pass. The question is not, "Will you start?" but "Will you finish?" Too many people start off well, but along the way they have some setbacks, get discouraged, and quit.

But God is called "the author and the finisher of our faith." He has not only given you the grace to start but the grace to finish. When you are tempted to give up on a dream, a relationship, or a project, you have to shake it off. If you will keep moving forward in faith, honoring God, you will come into a strength that you didn't have before, a force pushing you forward. That's finishing grace. That's God breathing in your direction, helping you to become who He created you to be.

1. Describe a challenge you are facing at the moment that you are tempted to quit. Where is the pressure coming from?

   ....

   ....

   ....

   ....

2. How do you think God wants you to respond to it?

   ....

   ....

   ....

   ....

When you were moving forward and taking new ground with a dream, a project, or a relationship, the enemy will work overtime to try to keep you from finishing. Don't get discouraged when you have setbacks, people come against you, or a negative medical report. That's a sign that you're moving toward your finish line.

It says in Philippians, "God began a good work in you, and He will continue to perform it until it is complete." One translation says, "He will bring you to a flourishing finish"—not a defeated finish, where you barely make it and are beat up and broke. You are coming to a flourishing finish, a finish more rewarding than you ever imagined.

3. When you face setbacks, put downs, or negative news, what are your immediate thoughts? Do they include what God is doing in your life?

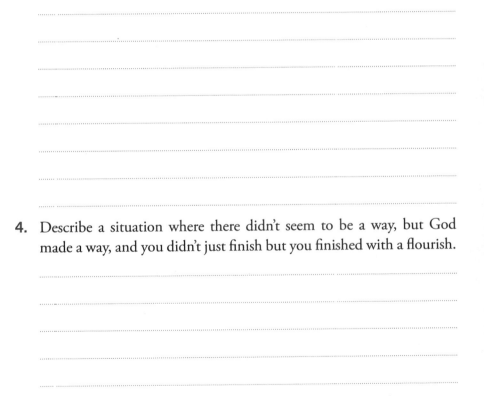

4. Describe a situation where there didn't seem to be a way, but God made a way, and you didn't just finish but you finished with a flourish.

As a teenager, God gave Joseph a big dream that one day he would rule a nation. But when Joseph was seventeen, everything went wrong. His brothers betrayed him and sold him into slavery in Egypt, where he was put in prison for years for something he didn't do. It looked as if his dream was dead. He must have been depressed, angry, bitter, and upset. Nothing had turned out right. But Joseph understood this principle. He knew he had the grace not only to start but to finish what God put in his heart. So he stayed in faith. He kept doing the right thing when the wrong thing was happening. And one day his dream miraculously came to pass.

5. When people do you wrong and situations look impossible, compare your typical response to that of Joseph's.

....

....

....

....

....

....

....

6. The next time that the going gets tough in your life, what are you discovering about God that gives you the power to overcome it?

....

....

....

....

....

....

....

....

The closer you get to your destiny, the tougher the battles become. The Scripture says, "As your days are, so shall your strength be." This means your strength will always be equivalent to what you need. If you were to get a negative medical report, you're going to have the strength to deal with it. You're not going to fall apart. Your strength will always match what you're up against. The psalmist said, "God is a very present help in times of need." In the difficulties of life, if you will get quiet and turn off the negative voices, you will feel a peace that passes understanding. You find that there is finishing grace for every season.

7. The next time that you face an overwhelming battle, such as dealing with the loss of a loved one or being laid off from your job, describe how you will find the strength to overcome what feels insurmountable. Write a plan for how you will tap into the strength of finishing grace.

> *God knows every hill, every setback, and every disappointment you're facing. He said that His grace is sufficient. You will never come to a hill where you don't have the strength to climb it.*

After many years of doing the right thing, sharing the good news, and helping other people, the Apostle Paul sat alone, in a dungeon, on death row. It looked as though God had forgotten about him. But Paul wasn't defeated, depressed, or feeling sorry for himself. Even though he was in chains, his enemies couldn't stop what God wanted him to do. Since Paul couldn't go out and speak publicly, he wrote book after book. "Here's a letter to the Ephesians, to the Colossians, to the Romans, to the Corinthians." He wrote over half of the books of the New Testament, much of it from a prison cell, and some 2,000 years later we still feel his influence. What Paul's enemies meant for harm, God used for good.

8. Describe a past difficulty that God didn't turn around the way you hoped and expected. How did you feel? Did it diminish your passion?

....

....

....

....

....

....

....

....

9. In the midst of those kinds of difficulties, how can you shine as a bright light and have God's favor as Paul did?

....

....

....

....

....

....

....

God didn't breathe His life into you, crown you with favor, and put seeds of greatness on the inside to start the race. He sent you to finish it. The Scripture talks about how the race is not for the swift or for the strong, but for those who endure till the end. You don't have to finish first. You're not competing with anybody else. Just finish your course. Keep your fire burning. You weren't created to give up. We can all find a reason to drop out of the race. We can all find an excuse. But you have to dig your heels in and say, "I am determined to finish my course."

10. When Paul came to the end of his life, he said, "I have finished my course." One translation says, "I finished my course with joy." What truths do you need to put in place in your life that will not only help you to live with joy today but to actually finish your course with joy?

There is a flame burning on the inside of us that Scripture says we must fan the flame and stir up the gifts. Finish your course with your fire ablaze!

CHAPTER FOURTEEN

I Am Strong
You Can Handle It

The Scripture says, "The rain falls on the just and the unjust." Just because we're a person of faith doesn't exempt us from difficulties. We all go through challenges, disappointments, and unfair situations. It's easy to let these overwhelm us to where we think, *This is too much.* But God would not have allowed it if you couldn't handle it.

In difficult times, you have to talk to yourself the right way. Have a new perspective. You are not weak. You are full of "can do" power. You are strong in the Lord. The Apostle Paul put it this way: "I have strength for all things through Christ who empowers me." Listen to his declaration: "I am ready for anything. I am equal to anything through Him who infuses strength into me." He was stating, "The enemy may hit me with his best shot, but it won't stop me. I'm more than a conqueror."

1. Paul faced a long list of difficulties on his missionary journeys—beatings, false accusations, shipwrecks, hunger, and imprisonment. Compare your typical reaction to life's difficulties to Paul's.

....

....

....

....

> *You can't have a weak, defeated mentality. You have to have a warrior mentality.*

....

....

The prophet Isaiah said, "Take hold of His strength." Every morning you need to do exactly that and declare, "I am ready for and equal to anything that comes my way. Almighty God has infused me with strength. He has equipped me, empowered me, anointed me, crowned me with favor, and called me to reign in life as a king." That's not just being positive. You're taking hold of strength. That's why the Scripture says, "Let the weak *say*, 'I am strong.'" When you say it, you're getting stronger. Shake off a victim mentality and have a victor mentality.

2. If you're always talking about your problems and lacks, all that's doing is draining you. What negative statements do you routinely make that keep you entrenched in a victim mentality?

    ....

    ....

    ....

    ....

    ....

    ....

    ....

3. Name an area of your life that you will take hold of God's strength today and declare you can handle it.

    ....

    ....

    ....

    ....

    ....

    ....

    ....

    ....

God is not going to deliver us from every difficulty. If He did, we would never grow. The Scripture says, "Our faith is tried in the fire of affliction." When you're in a tough time, that's an opportunity to show God what you're made of. Anybody can get negative, bitter, and blame God. But if you want to pass the test, you have to be a warrior.

Colossians 3 says, "God has given us the power to endure whatever comes our way with a good attitude." Dig your heels in and declare with Paul, "Nothing is a surprise to God. I can handle it. I'm ready for it. I'm equal to it. God is still on the throne. He is fighting my battles, and on the other side of this difficulty is a new level of my destiny."

4. How can you change your negative response to difficulties by changing your underlying attitude about difficulties?

....

....

....

....

....

5. Having the right attitude strengthens you to do the right thing when the wrong thing is happening to you. Apply that principle to a situation where someone is treating you wrong.

....

....

....

....

....

....

....

....

....

....

The Apostle Paul said, "We know that all things work together for good to those who love God." Friend, God is in complete control. You don't have to get upset when things don't go your way. You have the power to remain calm. Quit letting little things steal your joy. Every day is a gift from God. Life is too short to live it negative, offended, bitter, and discouraged. Start believing that God is directing your steps. Believe that He is in control of your life. Believe that He has solutions to problems that you haven't even had. If you will stay calm and stay in faith, God promised that all things will work out for your good.

6. Describe the last time you got upset when things didn't go your way.

7. Why is it that we get upset so easily and quickly when things don't go our way? What are we telling ourselves in those moments?

8. What should we be telling ourselves in those moments?

God has put an anointing on your life that seals you, protects you, enables you, and empowers you to handle anything that comes your way. He gives you strength when you don't think you can go on. He gives you joy when you should be discouraged. He makes a way when it looks impossible. Now we can all say with David, "Where would we be without the goodness of God?" Bottom line: God has equipped and infused strength into you. You are ready for and equal to anything that comes your way. When you face difficulties, remind yourself, "I am anointed for this. I can handle it. I know God is still on the throne. He is fighting my battles, and if God be for me, who dare be against me?"

9. Describe a situation in your life where you knew that God put an anointing on your life—where you had an inner strength or joy that enabled you to handle what you could never have on your own.

....

....

....

....

....

....

....

10. Reflect upon the role that the goodness of God has had in your life.

....

....

....

....

....

....

....

The Scripture says, "Do not be intimidated by your enemies." Don't be intimidated by that diagnosis. It's no match for you. Sickness cannot keep you from your destiny. God has you in the palm of His hand. Nothing can snatch you away. Don't be intimidated by that financial problem. Don't be intimidated by what somebody said about you. Greater is He that is in you than anything that comes against you. God has infused you with strength. The Scripture calls it "can do" power. When you press past what's coming against you, on the other side of that difficulty is a new level of your destiny.

11. What do you need to quit telling yourself that it's too much for you?

> *"I'm ready for and equal to anything that comes my way. I am strong."*

12. What positive results do you expect to enjoy as you tell yourself the truth that you can handle these matters?

CHAPTER FIFTEEN

I Am Anointed
You Are Anointed

We don't have to go through life doing everything on our own, trying to overcome challenges in our own strength, intellect, and hard work. We have an advantage. The Apostle John said, "You have an anointing from the Holy One." The anointing is a divine empowerment. It enables you to do what you could not do on your own. It will cause you to accomplish dreams even though you don't have the talent. It will help you overcome obstacles that look insurmountable.

In life's difficult times, you have to declare what Isaiah stated, "The anointing on my life is breaking every yoke." "The anointing is greater than this cancer." "The anointing is greater than this depression." "The anointing is causing me to overcome." Every time you say, "I am anointed," chains are broken. Fear has to leave. Depression has to go. Healing comes. Strength comes. Faith comes.

1. The anointing is only activated where there is faith. Write a declaration of faith that you are activating the anointing upon your life.

....

....

....

....

....

> *The anointing to us is like gasoline to a car.*

....

....

....

When David was a teenager, the prophet Samuel anointed him to be the next king of Israel, yet he spent years in the shepherd's fields after his anointing. The Scripture tells us to "reign in life as a king." You have a king's anointing, a queen's anointing, to live an abundant life, to accomplish your God-given dreams, to raise children who will be mighty in the land, to leave your mark on this generation. But on the way to your destiny there will be times of waiting where you have to be patient and keep doing the right things. You have to stay in faith and keep believing, *My time is coming. God has put the promise in my heart. I may not see how it can happen. But I have His anointing on my life.*

2. Do you feel you're stuck in a shepherd's field? Perhaps your work environment is negative or you're dealing with a difficult child or illness that never seems to change. Describe it.

3. Declare that the anointing on your life is breaking that yoke and that you will keep moving forward in faith and joy.

In the book of Judges, a woman named Deborah is described as "a mother in Israel." She didn't have an impressive position, title, influence, or prestige. She was a mom. Yet in a time of national crisis, Deborah knew God had put something on her that would cause her to excel. She took a step of faith that led to the liberation of her people.

How could this mother affect the whole nation? It was the anointing on her life. You are not limited by who you know, by how influential you are, or by how much income you have. There is something that supersedes talent, income, and experience. It's the anointing God has placed on your life. Quit making excuses as to what you can't do.

4. Deborah would have been considered "just a mother." Describe the "just"s that could be used as excuses to discount and limit you.

....

....

....

....

....

....

....

5. You are not "just" anything! You're a child of the Most High God. What has God put on your life that supersedes all of the "just"s?

....

....

....

....

....

....

....

....

....

There will always be negative voices that try to talk you out of your dreams and convince you to settle where you are, but you have a king's anointing. You've been raised up. You have what it takes. You and God are a majority. If you will start taking steps of faith, doing what you can, God will do what you can't. He will bring the right people and open the right doors. He will give you the wisdom and the creativity. He will make it all come together. You're going to step into that king's anointing, that queen's anointing. Paul said it this way. "Don't get tired of doing what's right. In due season you will reap, if you don't give up."

6. What are the negative voices in your life telling you?

7. When you hear those voices, what do you tell yourself?

8. Based upon your anointing, what will you tell yourself in the future?

David was anointed as king yet worked in the shepherd's fields for years in preparation for his ultimate promotion to the palace with untold favor, increase, and abundance in his life. I like how David put it in Psalm 23. He said, "God anoints my head with oil." He went on to say, "Because I am anointed, my cup runs over." When you walk in your anointing, knowing who you are and whose you are, at some point your cup will run over. You will see God pour out blessings that you cannot contain. Don't you dare settle in the shepherd's fields. Almighty God has anointed you. What He has spoken over your life will come to pass.

9. Revisit your shepherd's field. My concern is that you have already settled in with the sheep. Honestly address how you feel.

> *You were not created to barely get by.*

10. Jesus came that you might live an abundant life. You will see God pour out blessings that you cannot contain. Write David's declaration from Psalm 23, and put your name in it.

David was first anointed by Samuel, then years later by the men of Judah, and later the men of Israel joined the men of Judah and anointed him king over all of Israel. He could have told them he already had been anointed, but David understood the importance of having a fresh anointing. You can't win today's battles on yesterday's anointing.

Just as the men of Judah anointed David for his new season, I believe today God is releasing a fresh anointing in your life. You're going to go where you've never been and see negative situations turn around. Chains of addictions and bad habits are being broken. Healing, promotion, and restoration are coming. You're going to step into the fullness of your destiny. Friend, you have a king's anointing, a queen's anointing.

11. Write a prayer for a fresh anointing on your life that brings help, favor, wisdom, and breaks every yoke that hinders you from stepping into the fullness of you destiny.

When you pray, God will breathe freshness onto your life.

CHAPTER SIXTEEN

I Am Patient
Trust God's Timing

In life we're always waiting for something—waiting for a dream to come to pass, waiting to meet the right person, waiting for a problem to turn around. When it's not happening as fast as we'd like, it's easy to get frustrated. But you have to realize that the moment you prayed, God established a set time to bring the promise to pass. Understanding that takes all the pressure off. You won't live worried, wondering when this is ever going to happen. You'll relax and enjoy your life, knowing that the promise has already been scheduled by the Creator of the universe.

Here's where it takes faith. God promises that there are set times in our future, but He doesn't tell us when they will be. The Scripture says, "Those who have believed enter into the rest of God." The way you know you're really believing is that you have a rest. You're at peace. You know the answer has been set in your future and is on the way.

1. Describe your immediate response to this life principle as it relates to an issue that you are currently waiting for something to happen on.

Don't let the negative thoughts talk you out of it.

There are set times in your future. You've prayed, believed, and stood in faith. Let me assure you that you're going to come into set times of favor, a set time where a problem suddenly turns around, a set time where you meet the right person, a set time where a good break thrusts you years ahead. That's what Habakkuk said. "The vision is for an appointed time. It may seem slow in coming, but wait patiently, for it will surely come." Not, "maybe come." Not, "I hope so." God has already set the date. The appointed time has already been put on your calendar. One translation says, "It won't be one second late."

2. How do you feel about Habakkuk's declaration? What does that mean to you?

_____

_____

_____

_____

_____

_____

3. Do you trust God enough to believe that your set times are coming?

_____

_____

_____

_____

_____

_____

_____

_____

_____

_____

A great prayer we should pray every day is, "God, give me the grace to accept Your timing." We live in a society that demands everything right now. We're being programmed for immediacy. But the Scripture says, "It's through faith and patience that we inherit the promises." God can see the big picture for our lives. He knows what's up ahead. He knows what we're going to need, who we're going to need, and when they need to show up. If what you are asking Him for hasn't happened yet, instead of being uptight, have a new approach. "God, You know what's best for me. I'm not going to live frustrated. God, I trust Your timing."

4. On a scale of 1 to 10, with 1 being upset and impatient and 10 being patient, how would you grade yourself? Describe where you are at.

_____

_____

_____

_____

_____

_____

_____

_____

_____

5. What truths can you start believing that will help you improve your score?

_____

_____

_____

_____

_____

_____

_____

The Scripture says, "God didn't take the Israelites the shortest route to the Promised Land, because He knew they were not prepared for war." God could see the big picture. He knew that if He took them the shortest way, their enemies would be too powerful and they would be defeated. So on purpose, God took them on a longer route to protect them and to strengthen them so that they could fulfill their destiny.

God doesn't always take us logically from A to B to C. If something is not happening on your timetable, turn it over to God and say with David, "God, my times are in Your hands. I'm not going to worry about why something hasn't happened or why it's taking so long. I trust You."

3. Looking back, how has your timetable for things happening compared to when God actually brought them to pass? What wisdom can you take from that and apply to your situations today?

> *While you're waiting, don't make the mistake of trying to figure everything out.*

Our God is not a random God. He is a precise God. He has lined up solutions for you down to the very second. The time is set.

Sometimes when we get in a hurry, we make the mistake of taking matters into our own hands and trying to force things to happen. We end up missing God's best. This is what happened with Abraham and Sarah. God gave them the promise that they were going to have a baby, but when the promise was delayed, they tried to help God out. Don't be impatient, as they were, and go around birthing Ishmaels when God wants to give you Isaacs. It says in Psalms, "When you delight yourself in the Lord, God will give you the desires of your heart." There's a big difference between God giving you something and you having to work to make it happen. When we force things, it's a constant struggle.

7. Describe a situation in your past where you tried to force what you believed was the right thing. To what did you give birth?

....

....

....

....

....

....

....

8. How might the outcome have been different if you had waited in faith?

....

....

....

....

....

....

Your situation may be taking longer than you thought. Maybe it's something more difficult than you've ever experienced. So often we think we have to do it only in our own strength. This is when many people make quick decisions that end up only making matters worse. The Scripture says, "Be still and know that I am God." When you feel overwhelmed and you're tempted to take everything into your own hands, you have to make yourself be still. The battle is not yours. The battle is the Lord's. God is going to show His strength, His healing, His goodness, and His power like you've never seen before. Be still.

9. About what situation in your life is God saying, "Be still and know that I am God," right now?

When you remain at rest, Almighty God will fight your battles.

10. Write a declaration that you believing that God is going to give you the desires of your heart.

CHAPTER SEVENTEEN

I Am Forgiven

God Loves Imperfect People

Most of the time we believe God loves us as long as we're making good decisions, resisting temptation, and treating people right. But the problem with this kind of reasoning is that we all make mistakes. No matter how good of a person we are, there will be times when we don't perform perfectly, times when we have doubts, times when we fail. When we blow it, it's easy to think that God is far from us.

But when that happens, God loves you so much that He pursues you. He won't leave you alone until He sees you restored and back on the right course. He will express His love in a greater way. That's the mercy of God coming after you, saying, "You may have blown it and let Me down, but you're still My child. You may have lost faith in Me, but I haven't lost faith in you." Don't beat yourself up if you don't perform perfectly all the time. God loves imperfect people.

1. When you make a mistake, blow it, give in to a temptation, what are your immediate thoughts about God? Do you believe He turns away from you or He runs to you?

....

....

....

....

....

> *Sometimes religion pushes people down.*

....

....

Think about Peter. Despite being warned by Jesus that he would deny Him three times, Peter did exactly that at the moment when Jesus needed him the most as a friend, when He was at His lowest moment. No wonder the Scripture says, "Peter went out and wept bitterly." Yet after Jesus rose from the dead, Peter is the first disciple whom the angel instructs Mary Magdalene to tell that Jesus is alive.

God is saying to Peter as well as all the people who have fallen, the people who have made mistakes, "I'm not only alive, but I still love you. I still believe in you. If you will let go of the guilt and move forward, I will still get you to where you are supposed to be."

2. If God pursued Peter after his utter failure, how about you? Is there something in your life that you feel is beyond His forgiveness?

_____

_____

_____

_____

_____

_____

_____

3. What is God saying to you about any failure or mistake you have made?

_____

_____

_____

_____

_____

_____

_____

God's love is not based on our performance. It's based on our relationship. We are His children.

In the Scripture, it talks about "the God of Abraham, the God of Isaac, and the God of Jacob." Abraham and Isaac both seem to qualify, but Jacob doesn't make a lot of sense. Jacob was a cheater. He went around deceiving people. He stole his brother's birthright. Jacob was known for making poor choices. What was God saying? "I'm not just the God of perfect people who never make a mistake. I'm the God of people who have failed, who have blown it, and who have had a rough past."

4. Put your name into the Scripture, "I am the God of your father—the God of Abraham, the God of Isaac, and the God of _____." How does that make you feel?

> *You can't change the past. Learn from your mistakes. Keep moving forward.*

5. Even after Jacob changed his ways and God changed his name to Israel, God still called Himself "the God of Jacob." What does that tell you?

In the book of John, there was a lady who had been married five times. She was living with a sixth man. You could imagine the heartache and pain that she had gone through. I'm sure she felt beaten down by life—not really living, just existing. And yet Jesus told His disciples He must travel out of His way to express His love for her. She is known as "The Woman at the Well." It's interesting that the first person Jesus revealed Himself to as the Messiah was not the religious leaders. It was a woman who had made so many mistakes. That one encounter changed her life.

6. When you've failed and haven't measured up so many times, have you allowed the accusing voices to convince you that God is disappointed in you? Have you given in to condemnation and guilt? Are you now?

7. God is reaching out to you. His mercy is bigger than any mistake that you've made. Receive His grace and pardon and declare it here.

When Thomas heard that Jesus had risen from the grave, everyone was so excited—except Thomas. They were all believers, but Thomas was full of doubt. He had all these questions. Then one day he was in a room together with the other disciples, and Jesus came walking *through* the doors. They nearly passed out. What's interesting is Jesus bypassed all the people who had faith and went to the one person in the room who had doubt. He didn't chew him out, but rather He answered Thomas's doubts.

Notice the pattern. When you have doubts, when you blow it as Peter did, when you fail as the Samaritan woman did, God is not far away. It's just the opposite. God comes to the people who need Him the most.

8. Thomas doubted once, but has been labelled "Doubting Thomas." Have you done something that made you feel you are labelled for life?

....

....

....

....

....

9. Thomas is credited as being the one who brought the Good News to the entire nation of India. How does that encourage your faith?

....

....

....

....

....

....

....

....

> *God's ways are not our ways.*

Too often we get our performance mixed up with our identity. You may have failed, but you are not a failure. That's what you did. Failure is an event. That's not who you are. You are a child of the Most High God. You've been handpicked by the Creator of the universe. God is not judging you by your setbacks. Maybe you've blown a relationship, had an addiction, done something you're not proud of. Don't let that become your identity. You are free. You are clean. You are restored.

10. Friend, your sins have already been forgiven. Every mistake you've made and ever will make has already been paid in full. How can you stop replaying in your mind all the times that you've failed?

_____

_____

_____

_____

_____

_____

11. Dare to declare it: "I am forgiven. I am redeemed." Write it here, and what you are redeemed from.

_____

_____

_____

_____

_____

_____

_____

_____

If you'll shake off the guilt and receive God's mercy, you will not only live freer but you will still become all you were created to be.

CHAPTER EIGHTEEN

I Am Protected

You've Been Framed

When someone says, "You've been framed," we think we've been setup to look bad. But the Scripture talks about a different type of frame. It says, "The worlds were framed by the Word of God." It's not just talking about the physical *worlds*. The word in the original language is *eons*, meaning, "ages" or "times." It's saying that God has a frame around your times. He has put a fence, a boundary, around your life. Nothing can penetrate your frame that God doesn't allow. Trouble, sickness, accidents—they can't just randomly happen.

Not only can nothing get in without God's permission, but you can't get out. You can't make a mistake big enough to break out of that frame. It's a destiny frame. God won't let you get so far off course that you can't still fulfill your purpose. You may come right up to the edge, but you'll bump into the frame. God will push you right back.

1. What was your immediate response to this life principle? Write a list of practical implications that this principle entails for you.

Sometimes we're the most dangerous thing we face.

In the Scripture, David experienced this frame. He and his men had been protecting a rich man by the name of Nabal who had thousands of sheep. When Nabal foolishly insulted David in public, David was so furious that he planned to kill Nabal and his men. But Nabal's wife intervened and convinced him to stop. She was a part of the frame. God ordained her to be there at the right time, to know exactly the right thing to say. Had David shed innocent blood, that mistake could have kept him from the throne. David went right up to the edge, but he bumped into his frame.

2. Describe a situation in your life where you bumped into your frame and were kept from making a significant mistake.

....

....

....

....

....

....

....

....

3. David said, "Where would I be without the goodness of God?" He could have said, "Where would I be without this frame?" Where would you be without God's goodness and frame?

....

....

....

....

....

....

Jonah experienced the frame. God told him to go to the city of Nineveh, but he didn't want to, so he went in the opposite direction. You know the story. God will let you go your own way, but He is so merciful—at some point, you're going to bump into your frame. He let Jonah be thrown overboard, but He provided a fish as the frame. As with Jonah, you can run away, but you'll keep bumping up against it again and again. It will always push you back toward your divine destiny. The Most High God has fenced you in. He has put boundaries around your life so strong that all the forces of darkness cannot get in and you cannot get out.

4. Have you tried, as Jonah did, to run out of your frame, to run away from what you knew He wanted you to do and be? Describe it.

....

....

....

....

....

....

5. What the result of that situation? What wisdom did you gain from it, and how can you apply that to how you are living today?

....

....

....

....

....

....

....

....

....

In the Scripture a man named Saul was the biggest enemy of the church. He hated believers. He was having them put in prison, doing more harm to God's people than any person of that time. One day he was on the road traveling to Damascus and a bright light shone down on him, blinding him. A voice said, "Saul, why do you persecute Me? Don't you know it's hard to kick against the pricks?" God was saying, "Saul, it's hard to keep kicking against the immovable frame. There is a calling on your life, a destiny for you to fulfill, and it's not to stop My work. It's to advance My work." Saul surrendered to God's way and became the Apostle Paul, who went on to write over half of the books of the New Testament.

6. The Scripture talks about how God's calling is irrevocable. God is not going to remove the frame. What do you feel is His calling upon you?

7. How have you responded to God's calling? Have you surrendered to Him and set yourself to pursuing the dreams He has placed in your heart?

When I was ten years old, my eight-year-old sister, April, fell asleep on her float and drifted nearly two miles along the ocean shore in Hawaii, while our family desperately searched for her. She could have drifted out to sea or a thousand other bad things could have happened, but God had her in a frame. There was a boundary set around her.

Death can't penetrate your frame. God has to allow it. The number of your days, He will fulfill. When a loved one dies, no matter what their age, we may not understand why they pass, but we can know that the enemy doesn't have the power to take them. God called them home and received them into His presence. When Jesus rose from the grave, He said, "You don't have to worry anymore. I hold the keys of death." He was saying, "Nobody determines your time except Me."

8. When you understand this frame, you can say with the Apostle Paul, "O death, where is your sting? O grave, where is your victory? I'm not afraid of you. You can't defeat me." How have you viewed death?

....

....

....

....

....

....

....

....

9. Do you share Paul's declaration regarding death? Write it out and sign it. How does that make you feel when you declare it out loud?

....

....

....

....

....

....

When you go through tough times, you have a bad break, you're facing a sickness, don't get discouraged. Remember, the frame is still up. We see this principle in Job's life. Satan was looking for somebody to test. God said to Satan, "Have you seen my servant Job? There's none like him in all the land." Satan answered, "Yes, I've seen Job, but I can't touch him. You've put a hedge around him. If You take down the frame around his life, Job will curse You." The enemy can't just do whatever he wants. He has to ask God for permission. God has to allow him to do it. Job went through a time of testing. He fought the good fight, and in the end, not only did he not curse God, but he came out with double.

10. In the light of God's frame around your life, apply this powerful truth to whatever is worrying and stressing you. Be specific.

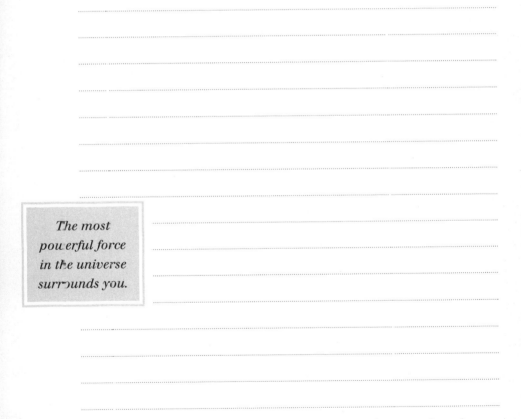

The most powerful force in the universe surrounds you.

Now all through the day, instead of worrying, under your breath, say, "Lord, thank You that my life has been framed, including my children, my health, my finances, my dreams, and my future. I am protected."

CHAPTER NINETEEN

I Am Generous
Become a Miracle

Many people are praying for a miracle. They're asking God to send them comfort in a time of loss, help with their children, or to provide them training or work. We can become the miracle they need. God will bring people across our path so that we can be the answer to their prayer.

You are a miracle waiting to happen. Somebody you know is lonely. Somebody got a bad medical report. Somebody is discouraged, saying, "God, send me somebody." You are that somebody. You can lift the fallen. You can restore the broken. You can be kind to a stranger. You can become someone's miracle. Life is so much more rewarding when you take time to become the miracle.

1. What was your first thought when you read this? How do you feel about being a miracle to others?

....

....

....

....

....

....

2. In what ways can you reach out to others and make a difference?

....

....

....

....

....

....

We know that God can do miracles. But He's also put miracles in us. We can be the answer to someone's prayers. You can be the good break they're looking for. You can be the help they've been longing to have. It may be just teaching your coworker the skills you know. Or helping that family that's struggling with the rent. Or taking that young man to baseball practice with your son each week. It's no big deal to you, but it's a miracle to them. It's what will push them toward their destiny.

3. What holds you back from helping others when you see a need? How can you instill this attitude of being a miracle waiting to happen?

Being generous involves far more than just your finances.

4. Someone you know has a need today that you can help with. Describe it as well as the steps you'll take to come alongside them with help.

Perhaps you are the one who needs a miracle. Here's the key. If you will become a miracle, God will always make sure that you have the miracles that you need. When you take time to invest seeds in others, the right people, the right opportunities, and the breaks you need will be in your future. God will get you to where you're supposed to be. That's what it says in Proverbs 11: "When you refresh others, you will be refreshed." If you want your dream to come to pass, help somebody else's dream come to pass. If you need a miracle, become a miracle.

5. Write an honest review of whether you think you're too busy to really help or invest in someone else.

6. You can't help everyone, but God has people in your path who are connected to your destiny. As you help them rise higher, you will rise higher. Name at least one person and how you can help them.

Jesus told a parable in Luke 10 about a man who was attacked and beaten by bandits and left beside the road, almost dead. Both a priest and a Levite past by and did nothing. Then a Samaritan man came by and became a miracle, carrying the man to a place of help and paying the costs. My question is: Which person are you?

When you get down low to lift somebody up, in God's eyes, you can't get any higher. The closest thing to the heart of God is helping hurting people. When you take time to restore the broken and wounded, encourage them, wipe away their tears, let them know that there are new beginnings—that's the religion Jesus talked about. And it provides opportunities for you to go to a higher level. Become the miracle.

7. It's easy to judge people and feel that because of their life choices that they don't deserve our help. What do you tend to do with those type of people in your life? Pass them by?

....

....

True religion gets dirty. It goes to where the needs are.

....

....

....

....

....

....

8. Anybody can find fault with others. What reasons can you find to get down and dirty and help love them back into wholeness?

....

....

....

....

....

....

....

When you see someone in need and feel compassion flowing out to them, don't put it off. Don't be a passerby.

We often don't realize we have the most powerful force in the universe on the inside. What may seem ordinary to us, no big deal, becomes extraordinary when God breathes on it. The Scripture says, "A gentle tongue brings healing." A phone call, giving someone a ride, taking them out to dinner, encouraging them in their dreams—there are miracles in you waiting to happen. Some people just need to know that you believe in them. When you tell them, "You're amazing. You're going to do great things," that may seem simple to you, but to the other person it can be the spark that brings them back to life.

9. Describe a situation where you did or said something to someone and it made an impact on their life in a way you never imagined.

....

....

....

....

....

....

10. What can you take away from that situation and apply right now in someone else's life?

....

....

....

....

....

....

....

....

Your destiny is connected to helping others. Isaiah put it this way. "When you feed the hungry, when you clothe the naked, when you help those in need, then your light will break forth like the dawn and your healing will quickly come." If you will make it your business to become a miracle, God will make it His business to give you miracles. Your healing, your promotion, and your vindication will quickly come. You will never lack His blessings and favor.

11. Write Isaiah's statement with your name in it.

....

....

....

....

12. Describe what you think your life would be like if God's light was breaking forth like the dawn and healing came quickly.

....

....

....

....

....

....

13. What can you do to make Isaiah's statement a reality in your life?

....

....

....

....

....

....

STAY**CONNECTED,**
BE**BLESSED.**

From thoughtful articles to powerful blogs,
podcasts and more, JoelOsteen.com is full of
inspirations that will give you encouragement and
confidence in your daily life.

AVAILABLE ON JOELOSTEEN.COM

 today'sW◯RD

This daily devotional from Joel
and Victoria will help you grow
in your relationship with the Lord
and equip you to be everything
God intends you to be.

 **Joel Osteen**
STREAMING

Miss a broadcast? Watch Joel
Osteen on demand, and see
Joel LIVE on Sundays.

 **Joel Osteen**
PODCAST

The podcast is a great way
to listen to Joel where you
want, when you want.

CONNECT WITH US

Join our
community of
believers on your
favorite social
network.

PUT JOEL IN YOUR POCKET

Get the inspiration and
encouragement of Joel Osteen
on your iPhone, iPad or Android
device! Our app puts Joel's
messages, devotions and more
at your fingertips.

Thanks for helping us make a difference in
the lives of millions around the world.